# The Touch

Also by Cynthia Kraman

*The Mexican Murals*
*Club 82*
*Taking on the Local Color*

# *The Touch*

## Cynthia Kraman

BOWERY BOOKS
BOWERY POETRY SERIES #7
YBK Publishers
New York

*The Touch*
Copyright © 2009 by Cynthia Kraman

Please direct all inquiries to:
Editors
Bowery Books
310 Bowery
New York, NY 10012

Bowery Books    Bowery Voices Series
Editors Marjorie Tesser and Bob Holman

Cover photograph by Abbot Genser
Cover design by Suzanne Altman

ISBN: 978-0-9800508-8-2

Library of Congress Control Number: 2008944374
Manufactured in the United States of America

Bowery Books are published in affiliation with
YBK Publishers, Inc.,
39 Crosby Street,
New York, NY 10013,
whose publisher, Otto Barz, is the inspiration for this series. With thanks to Bill Adler.

Bowery Books is the imprint of Bowery Arts and Science, a non-profit cultural organization. We are grateful for the assistance we receive from individual donors, foundations, and government arts agencies.


This publication is made possible with public funds from the New York State Council on the Arts, a state agency.

In loving memory of my mother
Esther Kraman (1922–2007)

The author would like to thank Maggie Balestreri, Barbara Crespo, Richelle Fiore, Joyce Jenkins, and Benjamin Kraus for their help in preparing this manuscript. Our proof reader Charlotte Carter's eagle eyes prevented many errors. Special thanks go to the brilliant Marjorie Tesser and the eternal bon vivant, Bob Holman, without whose kindness, generosity of spirit, and mad skills this book would not be, period. And of course a riot of kisses for Abbot.

# Contents

# SPEAK IN THE DARK

# Acknowledgments

## *SPEAK IN THE DARK*

"Visiting Haworth, Brontë Parsonage" appeared in *The Paris Review*.

"The Touch," "Speak in the Dark," "The Old Old Truth," and "Retranslating" appeared in *Western Humanities Review*.

"Summer Poem # 8" appeared in *The Café Review*.

"How Painful Is Birth, for Poets Too" is online at *Speechless the Magazine*.

"Speak in the Dark" is anthologized in *Bowery Women: Poems*.

"My Own Private Iditarod" appeared in *Poetry Flash*.

"Little Ginkgo," "No Noon But Mine, No Heat But Yours," "Summer Night Poem 1," and "Summer Night Poem 5" appeared in *Open City*.

"When Anger Is an Idol, I Lose" and "The Sluts of Delft" appeared in *PiF Online Magazine*.

"Ride to Manhattan" appeared in *The Paris Review*.

# Contents of *Speak in the Dark*

## *Little Ginkgo*

## *Winter Night Poem*

# The Touch

# The Touch

It built too long. It could not build so long
In me and be. It spawned new forms in me.
A paradise was joined with agony
A panda was conjoined with apish ways
A waning day combined with rosy night
It could not be. It clowned into the dark
It left a path of luminary junk.

I found a heap of clothes I couldn't wear
And walked them to the corner with the dogs.
Some homeless person with a fashion sense
Would wear or sell the clothes I couldn't wear.
I turned the laptop on and visited
A chatroom with incendiary scrawls
On hands and knees I scrubbed the chatter off.

I sent a fax. I sent an image off.
Its latency developed and dried off.
Did you ever touch a butterfly? Wings
That beat and dried against some cool green rock
By a lily pond? Did your touch
Ever ruin the creator impulse
And creation? Aviatrix, aviation?

# Summer Night Poem

When suddenly a cat yelps out loudly in heat
Outside the window of your rented rooms
Out on the sandy end of Long Island
(Rooms made not for sleeping or for living
By artists with a dominant aesthetic)
You will be glad the cat and the renters
Next door have sliced into your lakeside night

The renters are dreadful. A weepy girl
Summons all the breaking darkness of love
The cat devours the stillness of summer
You remember the ocean at your ankles
Wanting to drag you in and eat you
Luckily life has interrupted the stagy
Dawn shimmering across Fort Pond to your rooms

Your rooms hold your bags, your clothes, your two books
Your sketchpad, two beds, your mother
Beside you sleeping and breathing elfin
Breaths in the rooms you rented on Montauk.
The rush of privet and roses and ocean
Melting with lilies are yours, are gilded
By each meaty night's hundred undoings

# The Old Old Truth

My mother and her angers and the moon.
That was the evening, and that was the meal.
Her old old stories. Stories of the war.
Her old old guilt. Spewed across a moon
High up there as I tossed my head far back
To find a helpful word, but found a face
Instead, of mist and ash, like milk descending.

Are you ever lonely when you're not alone?
I was asked this question by a girl named Truth.
I tossed my head back sharply, felt the warm
Hands of the sun descending down my face.
But I was silent to my foreign girl
Who walked beside me with a crumpled step
So young to hurt but much too old for lies.

Isn't it truth that I offer to the warm
Warm body that I handle in my bed?
A body lies, a mouth coughs up, shuts down.
The probing tongue, the plumy eye, every
Digit thumbs its nose at truth. I cut
My finger to the quick prepping up for mom.
Our meal was small; we ate the greater lights.

# My Human Condition

If God loved me the way I loved God, then
I'd be a far Alaska, I'd be tar
I'd be the big toe of a sleeping foot
A broom, a bullet, useful. I'd be cream
For kitty, Johnny's nightlite. Or a scrape.
A TV station everyone could watch.
Old car. An apple. Sanctifying prayer

I'd put myself in God's hands like a pie
Ready to be cut up and eaten warm.
Nor heed the word of wasting in the wind
Nor know the doubter stamping in the lane
My heart and God's would beat together, then
No moody distance from myself or thou
No antiphonal reader and response

Then God would streak through me and me through God
A chunk of light, a cold spasmodic kiss
A dab of burning truth would lubricate
The passage of myself through what is not
No interference from a human brain
No beading sweat slopped on the brow of heart
No no, no yes, no needling in-between.

# Summer Night Poem

Sometimes the contours of love are not human.
My dog's snout, his long, lovely scrotum.
Ah! So soft! you're laughing. But when our eyes meet
It isn't lust, but the turbulence
Of love that thrills through me. The light is brighter
Around his head. His breastbone lifting lifts me.
I dream his lowness, I dream him tenderly.

And so much higher than my hand is God.
Lips soft of softest soft should meet mine
If this were the unstoppable thing.
God is so high, I should wear wings, I would
Have eyes like cannonballs to take him in.
But if this love is love it has no name.
Not any figure or sex, no close thing.

My pajamas are the leafy air
And night hush. It is July and the sun
Reached just this year its furthest point from us.
Is absence of the Heat of Noon relief?
Or that he returns from now on? Which is it?
I can't wait for the answer. I'm awake.
The murmuring air under my tongue, loves.

# Deep Song

Our terrible days need beautiful songs.
Our terrible days are terrifying
Because the most terrible of our demons
Has deserted us on the subway platform
And now we are just anybody. The demon has
Slipped under the opening express doors
And chosen a better poet to grin in.

The deep song of a small middle-aged
Fair-skinned Spanish woman, a voice
Drenched in sexuality and tenderness
Rumbling *cante jondo* in jazzy low
Leonine baroque riffs drifts
All the way down the platform. A layer
Of silky life—an atmosphere, an

Ozone of gardenia and red elegy.
Her chubby ringed fingers pluck and tickle
Her guitar and the terrible day
Is filled with a very human beauty.
Afterwards the emptiness like a chokehold
Returns, tightens, ties up the hollow heart
And the edge of things has its way.

# Speak in the Dark

O ocean's glassy waves, speak in the dark
O sticky countertops, speak in the dark
O uncollected thoughts, speak in the dark
O mountain, mouse, morass, speak in the dark
Running blood, ampersand, speak in the dark
Mossy stone, silent lark, speak in the dark
O remaindered poetry, speak in the dark

Faithless wives, small sharp knives, speak in the dark
O the dreaming succubus, speak in the dark
Telescope, rim of gold, speak in the dark
Let the narrow alleyway speak in the dark
Gleaming summer palace, speak in the dark
The great bell of heaven, speak in the dark
The prison and the park, both, speak in the dark

Gel and lacquer, lilies, speak in the dark
Antichrist, Christian, and the offending Jew
Cattleprod and rack, the whip, the arcade
Cooling streams, remorse, the agonized son
O repentant therapist, O large dogs
Single girls, skin of tooth, speak in the dark
Let the dead remembered, speak in the dark

## Summer Night Poem

You can learn the alphabet. You can learn
To write poetry. It won't help you much.
You will still enter the room surprised
To find pieces of paper waiting
For your inky self to slide wetly across them
You will be surprised to have to write more
Since you have already written a hundred years

You will even be surprised to be writing
At all. You expected to sleep. You took
Your hat off in the hall like a sales-clerk
And looked for aspirins, sedatives, speed
Before lifting the cover of a cooked meal
You made but didn't, couldn't quite get down
And left for yourself as another to eat

You can learn a new, different alphabet
Say of pictographs, computer graphics
And still it won't do you any good
You will never enter the lived present
Surprise will not lend you a silver straw
To sip life on the piazza. No, night,
Summer nights, you with your headache, you'll write.

# Wunderbar!

"Wunderbar." The rich German tourist sighs
And New York spills its wonderment for him:
A crowd of tourists lines Fifth Avenue
A corridor of flowers, lit, appears
And four performers make the night a stage
A dappled horse, his two front feathered feet
Up on the curb, takes in the German's gaze.
And this within a pause. He adds:

"Wunderbar." So wonderful, so complex
My natal town, my messy capital
Of pleasure for the learned wandering eye
To feed on nothing fixed, relentless flux
Of person, stone, arched tree. Of bus and bone.
A million doggy personalities.
A million boys, a million dazzling girls.

And me and him, the German, in the bus
His tall wife, skeptical and trousered, neat.
And later in the Village "Happy Birthday" sung
A cappella by a winsome trio
Into one cell phone. And a World Series
Played by both our teams. It's so—Wunderbar.
We feed it well; it keeps us wondering.

# Skating

All night I dreamt of flying in your arms
Careening, like a Christian, heavenward
But the erotic layer of the cold
Ejected paradise, and me, and you.
Then we were left, two skaters in the fields
As evening fell like lilac parasols
As evening fell like lists of saved and not.

As I flew in your arms you held me fast
Across your chest, a layering, a cross
And I held on like saviors do to God
And lay myself extended, like a cross
Of gold against your breathless magnitude
Your soft good hands held mine, your cheek of fire
Was pressed on mine. And there we died of bliss.

Then I woke up. I woke a few more times.
I woke up comfortable and warm and mad.
Both angry and insane. The bullets flew
From wall to wall and set the sheets on fire
And smoked the walls. I lingered in between.
The bandits had arrived, angelic hordes
To kill the inward eye. That Eden whore.

# Drinking with Lions

When the zebras head down to the drinking hole
The zebra kith and kin trot alongside
Each other looking like regular verbs
And the gnu, too. But when the lions
Come down, the king and all his killing tribe,
They come as separate parts of speech: the noun
For him, his verbal children, his descriptive

Wives lower their heads and tipple after
Scattering the harmless hairless crowd.
So say you were born in obscurity
Like me or you, but were a lion anyway.
You knew it from your lineage of heroes
From the way the sunset lit your head
Drinking in Africa, or up on a wall.

You knew you were a lion because you
Slept a lot and roared over nothing.
You knew it because you were a target
And a trophy and because the tamer types
Ran like hell. But any bully can say that.
Your real clue was that language and your body
Were old friends who enjoyed variety.

# *My Own Private Iditarod*

# My Own Private Iditarod

If we want the world to glisten like blonde
Women turning in a doorway, like thick
Issuings out of open mouthed bank vaults
Like boyish breakings: locks picked, dishes dashed
Like girlish dervishings: whirlwind of fire
If we want that we have to launch north, go
For the Iditarod of the soul. We

Have to make our twosome ragged loopings
Over the white snow of the fugitive
Present moment whose virginal nose goes
Sniffing along the ice's underbelly
For a track, trail. Tails erect we have to
Plunge deeper, snouts snarling, open, barking
Over the great expanse of terror.

Why? Because Michelangelo, writing
To his lover explained this: shattering.
That to love is to break. Like gold's mold
A lover must be entered by the other
And broken. Vision, art, all love just that.
For us, to harness all hot desires
To one. Then to race it in a cold world.

# No Noon But Mine, No Heat But Yours

No noon but mine, no heat of noon but yours
As our equators slice the day in two.
No moony missing parts but we eclipse
Together—that's rule one!—no partial, small
Eclipsing either—listen—no nuptial
I'll go shopping, you do the cleaning up—
We both shop. Then it's both down on our knees.

My universe of pain your universe.
No north your south, no trading east and west.
When my storms gather, thunder on. And when
You feel a fine ice setting in I freeze.
Go south, I glare a solar eye at you
Go sleeping, dreams crash headlong in our bed
Go writing, get your language at our bank.

Get pissing drunk, I'll drink you down the drain
And nag for nag, and headpats, one for one
Then I come crying—I drown in your tears
Until mice float like deadmen, ten toes up.
We make the earth one thing and many, then
A sudden saintliness occurs to you.
I'm peace itself. The cosmos breathes relief.

# I Hasten Burning

after a sonnet by Michelangelo Buonarrotti

I hasten burning to find myself under your eyes
I hasten burning to find myself again
I hasten to find myself again burning.
Burning, I hasten to find your eyes
I hasten to find myself under your
Burning eyes, to find myself burning
To burn myself again, under your eyes.

When I undo myself I always say
"To be is to be seen" (which I believe)
With which you agree. As you agree with:
"When we're apart we are still together."
Michelangelo wrote: "I hasten
Burning to find myself again under
Your eyes." Hastening to find he's found himself?

To be beneath eyes? Which is it, really?
To need the ocular ratification
Of the unburnt other watching from the woods?
To be burning with anticipation?
To self-destruct in the imminent blink
Of appearing before another stripped?
To feel the final fire of being known?

# The Night Mare

Because a haunted energy coupled
With an anger, a glorious head
Came foaming over both our bodies bent
(A crescent of horse head over a fence
Made out of ourselves, circling, and hunted)
And then because of all the spit and foam
We thought we were swimming. But we were dead.

Dead in our fear frozen into arcs
Used as a jump for the nightmare to clear
Dead in the trough of a negative space
Death likes to jump on a white snowing night
She glitters in bridles of diamond, of gold
She rides to our bodies and jumps fast and low
We feel her hooves dragging against our sad bones.

Now the night noises come tenderly back
The owl and cricket and velvety mouse
The slow-growing mushroom, the great female hawk
We whisper—is it safe to get up now?
We rise up like babies just opening our eyes
We feel for each other through mud and through blood
You are hurt. I am wounded, a little.

# When Anger Is an Idol, I Lose

I wanted God, God wanted me; we played
The azure was a great expanse of bliss
In those hard arms I whimpered with delight
And day shook all my anger out of me
And then the night came at me, sliding close
Where lack of God had left a hermit's hole
It ate and drank, and made me drink and meat

God smelled of you. The heavy sweat of love
Came endlessly. The kisses were alike.
The grabbing airless hope all had your name
Embroidered on its heaving, emblemed form
The wants were yours, the having and the lack
Stitched evenly in letters spelling: NAUGHT
And others spelling: NIGHT IS LIVING HERE

Now night, now anger, turn me on their spit
Until I see both you and God again
Me praying, me professing, walking, still
Me in the Natural History Museum
A tour guide for postmodern months and years
Me waiting for the message on the screen
To say "FORGIVEN" in a steady light

# The Sluts of Delft

The great imaginary spaces that they built
Those painters of the early school of Delft
Made emptiness the deity and placed
A pissing dog, a sucking child and nurse
As emblems of the damned organic life
Like fisheyes at the foot of marble walls
So small, so insignificant, alive

The bad hot girls of Delft had visitors
In small hot rooms made warm by silk and fur
Upon their bluish breasts so slightly flushed
Reflected in the Venus pearls they wear
In each recumbent tender tinted ear.
Their glassy eyes bend silently on space
Their pearly teeth part tenderly in smiles

How often is it inward, this bought flesh
When painted by Vermeer or by de Hooch
Two masters not of light or space or line
But of the flight of what is flesh and love
Into these girls who hold the only hint
Of an imagination filled with more
Than snarling spaniels, hunger, empty space

# Summer Night Poem

I have been writing/waiting for forty/fifty years, and more,
Always godscup and goldenbore heralding
Some sonata of the day; made-up
Flowers crowning an imaginary head.
The head my own, the flowers too my own.
The sonata given to me like toast—
On the side. The day, and something with it.

The day is really the point of it all.
Offering the sisterlings I saw sitting
Shoulder to shoulder on the subway bench
One tall and spare the other round and moist
Sitting at an immaculate angle
To the seat, both breathing into a middle
Distance as if augury might tumble in

At the next stop. Or having lunch with you.
Or riding the deliberate bus down Fifth.
Oh—all the faces of my New Yorkers
Rush at me, they pass me by, they come close
And leave with a hollow roar which is the
Underbreath of the city that ends up
Whacking us into words, writing us out.

# When at the End of Fifty Fierce Winters

When I sit on the stoop and winter
Frames figures with airy aureoles like
Workworld robots or humans so similar
That they are only head, long leg, two arms
Throwing commensurate shadowy
Worldworks to the floor of the city block,
Then I recount a particular day.

Against the supersaturated blue
Wind of the world I set my eye
Inside me and recall, recall, recall.
There my hand touches the velvety door
To dark Payard. There everyone drinks down
Hot dark thick chocolate from their cups
Like immigrants who hold with both their hands.

Then I recall two arms. I recall a voice.
"I've found you, found you in the week we'd lost,
Felt lost, grieved lost, wept lost. And here you are."
And in recalling that lost day, December
And every hope lost and the loss choking me
And then me found, and in recall refound
And in refound remade, remake my love.

# To You If Then Comes

O sweet my mine, if I get sick again
O guide me then, when winter storms in me
O navigable hours, when you made fast in me
O harboring time, and there we married up
And made two twin, to tumble in the waves.
Unfurled, the land! The arable, the dry
The old and torn, the beautiful and formed.

Come resurrect our sights, our sighing charts
Come sit beside, come show it all to me
Come touch the dimpled satin kissless lip
Come touch the touchless, light the sad unlit
Come climb my masted heart unwandering
And rearrange an ended calendar
And re-begin departures on wide seas.

When pain has reached its unknown outer rim
When I cry out, come cover up my mouth
Cover up my eyes, my mouth my moving tongue
My heated little limbs, my lamby parts
My cold hard ribs, my salty toes and tips
With you with you, with you my other best
And hold and hold and hold and hold and hold.

*Retranslating*

# Retranslating

All night I rearranged the ancient tongues
So that they spoke in quick translated rhymes
The ancients who had spoken tossed and turned
And murmured loudly, great trees of my dream.
The rain came down. It fell through me like words.
Its patter was as ancient as the rhymes.
And it translated me into myself.

This morning there is coolness. Coolness comes
A ringing sound, a waterfall, a winter
Wash of waters down the hills. The grey
Is radiant, feeding, feeling comes
Into me after freezing through the night.
First fingertips buzz, and then the rosy hand
Unclenches, and then, as she said, (but differently)
    "then the letting go."

I turn my hand before my face. It moves
Like Galatea's, loved into a blush.
I touch the crust of toast, I lift the cup
I drink a morning sip. It seems
An Etna on my tongue. The rain still falls
And still the ancient languages flow out
Retranslating in torrents, tender, tensed.

# Ride to Manhattan (with Rainbow)

Crossing the land in a train, I passed through
The borderless townlets of sprawled New York
Rising red brick out of nothing after
Low, slatted wooden houses shot forward
And schools, hospitals slid on. All the while
A patch of color hung in the evening sky
And the train rumbled against my shoes.

It was just a little square of light, not
A covenant or flag or great banner
But the postage stamp of a country deep
In continuous war, on a tear-stained
Envelope sent by a lover with great
Hands and a head of iron and dust
Whose feet rested hard on the rumbling earth.

We trundled the bridge. The sky expanded.
The patch broke and spread and drained down a long
Plume of smoke. Night's lights came on in the dark.
And as I was watching, something surged up
Under my feet and rolled against my heart.
The train sloped gently into Grand Central.
There was concrete beneath me, flesh beside.

Keats' House
Hampstead Heath


You arrive at the house of the poet
With the saddest story in the world.
He never had enough money, his brother
Had TB and had to be helped and held
Until he died in John's arms. Even the tree
Where he heard the Nightingale now has a sign
"This plum tree has been planted where John Keats

Heard the nightingale, in another tree."
The bed you lie your head on is not the bed
Where John coughed arterial blood, saying,
"I know the color of that blood, it is
My death warrant" as calmly and as gently
As you place your head on the pillow not his
Or the bird sings in a phantom tree at dusk.

The house is white and plain outside, most things
Are gone except for his writing desk, a chair.
All the portraits show a face that never
Felt the agony of love, the terror of death.
They all saw him, even close friends, as
Gentle resignation in human form
Not that first fierce thing trying to be born.

# Madness in Grasmere

The world is mad, even the fells are mad.
That's what they call these bare volcanic hills
Slamming against the sky with green and brown
With rocks and bracken, tiny clutching trees
They rise up like an aria then dwell
Heavily and moodily and great
So I am mad, and moody, and not great

The sheep are silly here, even insane
They wander up Helvellyn in a daze
Snorting up the bracken which is bitter
And grows madly, cigarettes for sheep.
They are lost, utterly lost. Then dogs
Bring them down. Then they get lost again.
So you are mad, and fear you'll wander, lost

The air is mad. One minute it is full
Of poppies and pinks, of roses and hay
And next it's full of dung and roaring jets
And the words of humans which are really mad
And fly right into mad, filthy ideas.
Thoughts which desire to be pink roses
But are mad. And that's the way it is here.

# Visiting Haworth, Brontë Parsonage

When I went up to Haworth there was peace
Between my teeth. An ordinary heart
Beat. My ordinary hands moved easily.
I heard my small train kill the simple air
The choke was on, the hit of steel to steel
The train pulled out of Leeds and started north
The little stops rolled by like heads chopped off.

This country is full of sheep and shining moors
Of houses climbing grieving up the hill
Of strange sad women writing fairytales
Their siblings falling down about like knights
Bleeding in beds from fever and TB
Cold in the schoolroom, dressed in white or grey
Cold in their beds, clutching their slim cold pens.

Charlotte was one who made it to the crown
And wore it once and dying put it down
And Emily, who never got that far
At twenty-nine she caught a cold and died.
I saw the room she went in, saw the couch
I touched its glossy arm, alarms went off
Then I went down from Haworth with her heart.

# When I Loved You/Grasmere/Haworth

When I loved you the cows raised up their heads
When I loved you the sheep came down the slopes
The good dog Pip came over and stood guard
Our kitten Velcro stretched along the rock
And curled her claws and caught the sun in them
When I loved you their Zoe ran the fields
And slew a dragon with her dragon sword

When I loved you the sun shone in our skin
The local sweets were hot under our tongues
When I loved you our drugs all worked and drink
Was gold Glenfiddich, and the golf was on.
Our pub was always at the end of walks
And Gareth always made our table snug
And we drank Jennings as the night came on

When I loved you we went up Haworth way
Past Bingley, Skipton, Keighley and the like
A local matron said she "hated it"
But stayed to play the Bingo and get laid
Diane from Newcastle served us steaming plates
As fuel after hiking Helvellyn's heights
When I loved you the world gave over, once

# Helvellyn

We made Helvellyn love us in July
The day we climbed her in an infant joy
We were all bright beginnings, light steps up
And sandwiches and water, KitKat bars.
We portaged love, that boat that two must lift
So that although we seemed to travel light
We dragged an awkward burden up the hill.

Or mountain, call it mountain. It is that.
It welcomed us, it stretched our lungs and legs.
We walked the steps that pack-horse ponies picked
And said hello to workers from the Trust
And to their dog, and to a man we saw
Who climbed Helvellyn in black woolen pants
For penance or for pleasure, who could tell.

Helvellyn's head came twice like twinning bliss
And at the top we stood at Striding Ridge
And read where Scott had seen the faithful dog
With Wordsworth. He who'd stayed three months up there
To guard his master's dead and broken bones.
Our poor young love! We laid it on the hill
And let Helvellyn have its way with us.

# The Pet

I woke up dreaming that I went to you
And you were owner of a little bird
A little yellow thing that trilled at me—
A thrilling trill—and then it fell asleep.
It sat upon its perch within the cage
And made a lemon color on the wall
We knew it was our love. We let it sing.

When we woke up the yellow bird was there
But quiet, like a little plastic bird.
I was uneasy; did it have to live
Inside a cage? And eat the same old seed
That all birds eat? And live like that, locked up
And on a perch, with mirror, bell, and beak
Reflected once, and so often asleep?

I saw its eye. Its eye was stony, round
And could not keep itself from seeing me.
And trilling out expected ecstasies.
But then the stupor, then the slaughtering sleep.
And so I fed the bright bird to the cat
And let the cat be torn apart by dogs.
Then we were sad. But we were better off.

## Five Roses

Five roses try to speak to me of death.
Oh canisters of light! Five roses lit at night.
"Death is a winking after a little splash
Death is a rouging of the cold wall's core
A monster, a minute, a swinging door
It can be so refreshing, a waterfall
The rough stuff, the gunshot, the old flashing foil."

Five roses try to speak of poetry
Out of the night, lit up on their pikes
Five little heads, a garden full of talk
Screaming like mice popped right through and caught.
"This is the way that poetry is made:
You cut off your head and speak and speak for days.
Then the writing's done. Then it can be read."

Five roses try to speak about a life.
Five silent balls are bobbing on their stems.
Nothing is delivered from their online site
Although I gave my card. I finally get a note:
"We cannot speak, we cannot yet describe
Something as odd as to be, like you, alive."
There were some petals in the envelope.

Summer Night Poem
Post-9/11 Frankenstein Monsters

I am not able to remain engulfed
By lightning. The (autonomy) (autocracy) of the soul,
Like a seamstress using a hatchet for
A needle, uses bolts of natural light
And the accompanying heavy thunder
To try to tie me up, down, or together
But has only smothered me, albeit

With the iridescence of (cosmic) (comic) junk.
Let me say it much more plainly: One day
While I was experimenting with how soft
A thing a human heart could be and beat
Which was an experiment using my own
Heart and another's quite soft and lovely
Both rolled pell-mell, into heaven or hell.

Wherever we were, inertia shimmied.
It kept us spinning. Finally we lost sight
Of each other, if hearts have eyes (they do)
And then I said, Oh no, make it otherwise!
And it was—the world bent—catastrophe
Apocalypse, falling angels, burning towers.
This universe cannot accommodate love.

# Lime

Lime Lime lines lined linked linked linked
Lunatic Lunatic Lunatic
I could not sit and wait for time to heal
My wounds were bleeding out and I felt cold
I hadn't eaten anything but limes
The nothingness of life was greeny, tame
I wanted golded limbs I wanted wild

I wanted and I wanted and I
Wanted something life refused to give.
Life sculpted a great ladder in my heart.
Each time that I began to climb its height
Each rung broke underneath my naked foot.
It hurt my heart sometimes to feel the break
Beneath my trusting foot. I tried ten times.

"You live in grief, Professor" one kid said
To me before my heart was broken through
Because I knew my sweetheart was quite done
With him, myself, the love, the life, the love...
Why not? Why not debrief one's life of love?
Why not refuse the smiling limey tears?
Why not release the lunatics to God?

## One Past the Whale—
## Nantucket—The Weathervane

One past the whale. Three quarters of my life.
Me mum is good she bothered me this morn.
Dad's gone, sis is in the dunk, her pool is
Sad, reflecting. The weathervane spins out.
The Law I lost's a revel, the revelry
Is lusterless. Come and come my lovely one
My loved and beloved one, to me.

You are the homeless home I wander in.
Marked by morning, suffering. Evening bears
Its heavy horses towards me to drink.
Hardly meaning—hardly boundaries! Hardly
Markers. Whales on houses, sharks on beaches
Eaten, eaters. This my mother taught to me.
No one gets away with it and lives.

Everyone is eaters, eaten. Self mess.
Loathing. Separation. All the pathless
Eagerness of youth is desperation.
The crow eats the dead, is made for the job.
The dead to be eaten, that is her job.
Be dead, be born, be beached, leak blood, rise up.
Be red. Be naked, knuckled under. Squirm (*struck through*) Live.

# How Painful Is Birth, for Poets Too

"The heart stops." Overheard once on the street—
The doctor, with her stethoscope and whites.
But long before, the brain is dead. That's true.
I saw my neighbor's husband die last week.
He breathed awhile after his brain was gone
And other organs, one by one they went
And then the heart, old trooper. It stopped too.

But on the other side of that long haul
Begins another process: Lighting up.
A cigarette. Having a coffee. Shots
Of something acrid, acid, something hard
Like loss and pain, like illness, like a wound
Or dread or death or any killing news
And there you go: gestation, birth, the wail

Of words on paper. Orderly and fixed
They stand up on the warped and wobbling page.
And then the pleasure—ah! I made it go
Without a beating heart I made it go!
I made it make a new and better heart!
A language heart, eternal. But it runs
On that old thumping, dying, human, heart.

*Little Ginkgo*

# Little Ginkgo

There we were. You and me. You and me and
Eternity. Endless airless soundless space.
Pagoda of light. Pagoda like room.
Who loves life in an empty tomb? Who dark?
Who loves lack? Who loves kneeling in the snow?
Wherever we race, wherever we go
Nothing but the miles, the declining sun.

Pagoda of light. A tree in the street
Burnishes me like an effigy
Melts my ringed finger with its trumpetings
Ravishes the others into golden arms
Little ginkgo, little ginkgo, please kiss me!
Each one prays loudly to the little tree
But the little tree is kneeling fast to Time.

Here we are. You and me. You and me and
Eternity. Warming, ordered, coursing space.
Pagoda of light!—Pagoda like room!
How I loved you hard in that witless room
Signed for by the hour as if we bought time
And not endless longing, not ecstasy
The electric unfamiliar of eternity.

# Summer Night Poem

August 14-15, the blackout

You might think a night without electricity
Would be dark and quiet, finally. But
It turned out to be full of sirens, voices
Screaming nasty laughter. It's so lonely
To be forced to be together. It's jail.
Without the hum of electricity
We changed, and others changed, and the night changed

Heat and fear made everyone party-mad
Drinking up the less and less cold beers
Madly barbecuing meat and fish
Thawing since 4:21pm
Ramming batteries into radios
As though one loud roar would make us happy
Or at least drown out the howling dogs

The dogs knew it was all wrong, and the birds
Dawn came up without a peep or wing
Fluttering into the roses. The roses
Curled in the heat and died on their stems
I couldn't sleep or read. I let two
Battery-run TVs die down, and my flashlight.
And the darkness, now different, was dumb

# City of God, City of Love;
# the Little Foxes

It was the end of summer. I had lived
Fifty winters as the City of God.
There it is all Justice, rubbed oatmeal fine
There all tables turn on consequence.
This much for serving as the house of the dead:
Fifty years of life with a hellfire mouth
Heart of milk, sex shut, a nautilus mind.

It was the end of summer. I have lived
Fifty winters as the City of Love.
There it's all beds sprung in the canopy
Airy tables set in the clustered grapes.
My body earned a body with its laboring
In the valley of the vineyards of the Name
Whose one kiss can annihilate four worlds.

But outside in the snow I hear quick boots
Crunching the perimeter, see the glint
Of your six-shooter sizing up my soul.
I hiss an invitation, I crook an agile thumb
But you are guardian and you creep without.
The cunning little foxes are not safe from you.
Oh come and kill them! Make me promised land.

# Winter Night Poem
## *I Am My Own Wife*

When winter is almost over and snow
Is a tenuous hug from a dying love
And the steam heat that rose in moaning notes
(Like a coven or choir) made us sigh,
Relax our limbs, so cold, under the blankets
(The heat's coming on less as the days get long)
Then we remember the beautiful ice.

But it was harder in the heart of it.
It was less charming battling down Broadway
To see a play and even indoors wear mittens.
Or take our chances with the rest of New York
Out there hailing taxis in thigh high whiteness.
But wasn't it wonderful the way the light
Burst blue and pink around each head and hand?

And wasn't it worth the frozen-footed
Ride in the grim coffin of the Six line?
We talked about how the actor did all that.
And you asked what it meant, "I am my own wife."
I suggested he was so absolutely
*Sui generis* that there was no Other.
Like ice he or she was its own mystery.

## "The Wray"

All night I spent wrapped in your absent arms
Emitting sounds an ocarina makes:
A little instrument, a little sound.
That was a night of years, I spent them small
I spent them in the cellar of the church
With all the other mice, so musical
We trembled with the organ through the floor

Then half of you took me off to the show
To see the Chardins—"The Wray," "The Soap Bubble"
And all those married hares and partridges
Who bleed, castrated, in each other's arms
The bird's legs splayed, the hare's soft nose all blood
As if he sniffed the sexual wound before
His own destruction came as he cried out

And every time we stopped you lay your lips
On mine and kissed me in your present arms
And I emitted whimpers at each squeeze
As if I were a music box, you said.
A box like that's not played, just opened up
And girl delights to hear herself in notes
And gasps out "oh" until the lid is shut

# The Scrim

When we were curious—my twin eye and I
We watched the neighbors through an opening
The neighbors were two women, sisters, old
Once married to the same hilarious man
Consecutively—and one had his son
Who married, and they all lived there as one
Family, in front of a pure white scrim.

The scrim was temporary—so were they
But back and forth they walked, all doing things
Or seemed to. Nothing certain. But they walked
Back and forth before the phantom wall.
They carried, carefully. They lay and slept.
They sat quite still. But separately, as if
They were one actor playing patience out.

Our eyes were carried with their carrying
And paced their paces, ate the bloodless meals
Erased of longing by their longingless
And watched their dumbshow from beyond their well
Of dryness—dry hair, long dry history
Of being someone substitutable
For someone not quite you but still, still you.

# Lines from Another Avatar, with Martini

You added, "the train is meant for people
like you ... mmm ... like us." But what separates us
from the rest of blind creation? Knowing
that to pour out one's life in a bar
is a good astringent to the wound
of pride, especially the next morning?
O shower! O infinite gratitude!

But not, not yet. Now, to be reading bad verse
on the subway is a substitute
for dreamland ... or for being the enviable
gods who enjoy their unformed darkness. ...
I always hated being the one who
left the end of the glass, the discussion
unworked out, all chaos. Wild metal roars on.

In the evening the mailbox is a desk
and the napkin a letter to answer
a pause, an unspoken, undated remark.
"I did like, little friend, to have been part
of your evening, that like a farewell
to the day, I just evaporated
and recondensed somewhat later, downtown."

## All About Us

I want to sit on either side of you
And play with you until you scream out "Stop!"
All day the weather pressed on us like weights
Severe and honest—hold them there and feel
How cold they are and how good torment feels
When nothing else is offered. Realize
How loath I am to let you up for air.

The ice is fine, its filigree licks out
A pattern on the walls my prison makes
Cat's coffin? Frump? Spinwasher?
Scholar's dish? Outmoded, bearded foreskin?
Rehearsed my lines? Forgot them? Wrote them down?
Broke down? Broke even? Bashed our head in two?
Come sit between us, let us answer you:

How can these questions mean when no one spoke?
How can the answer come when listening
Is painful, and the peal of thunderdash
And churchbell, sweet, both make us hold our head?
We want to redirect the hour of doom
From all the programs—set the pigeons free!
And pogroms, stop them, and the firewall.

# Abeyance

Everything that is me is in abeyance
Except for the electric heart. It beats
Against your downy leg at dawn.
In the wet crevice of God's mind, it beats.
Against the visible, it beats, it beats.
It beats against the big dealness of day.
It beats, it beats, it beats, it beats, it beats.

If you who are dead are waiting for me
To wake you up you are in for a long wait.
I am waiting myself. In the meantime
The body which once animated a motorcyclic stretch
Of highway, the beautiful eyes and neck,
Are lost among the almond blossoms of paradise
Which have grown up from your bodies, you dead
Who wish to break into my house and wake me.

You do not smell bad! It's the blossoms I smell.
My mechanical heart beats out their odor.
Look—if it's a thing that just thuds along
Why do I want so much to tear it out?
At the turn of a key my life is over.
Someone enters; the house is occupied.
The heart heaves. Even waiting, it has to beat.

# *Winter Night Poem*

# Winter Night Poem

O clear winter light I envy you
Bathing everything equally in moonglow
Putting a big blue tip atop each house
Like a cold nose high in the tottering sky
From which the eyes of the dull winter night
Stare down without blinking into the street
As if targeting all scurrying blood.

I envy you because you'd never be left.
Never be forgotten in the heart's planning.
Or if you were you wouldn't mention it
Because you'd be busy assassinating
Hope and her marvelous cousins the cats,
And rats, the nocturnal beasties and my own
Bare heart held aloft in the light like bait.

How divine to be divinity itself
Or its reflection—or would that be less
Even than me? Would a wooden soldier
Defend himself against autonomous light?
Refuse to cast a shadow? I see mine
Cast across the page like a crab moving
Sideways, in the same place only further along.

## Summer Night Poem

The night before a funeral is a thoughtful
Night. You think about dying. You imagine
Yourself in black, walking with others in a
Cemetery shining white and ancient
Like the forehead of an aging child actor
Who has turned to his image on the TV
And turned it off and tried to forget it

You try to forget there will be a coffin
And in the coffin the body of someone
You knew and liked in another younger life.
How handsome he was! How well she cooked!
There will be nothing like them under the sun
Except everyone else and their sister
Because we are all so terribly the same

Or am I just tired of people dying
People I know, and people far away
In worldwide urban battlefields. People
Who were just taking a walk or a bus
Who were planning to read an article
That would help explain why they died right now
During this lovely, bosomy summer night.

## My Apollonia

We were to explore the caverns of Dis
The high peaks of Jove, the hotspots of Cannes.
We had bought some fab gear—new bodies, new hats
Books on lassoing, on doodling in Catalan
Protocol for royalty and later, their footmen.
Urdu and Latin—we had our dictionaries
And signing for "more" in seventy tongues.

Then you decided you owed something, cash
To all the garage guys and your friendly play wife
So I waited and waited, but the debt
Just got worse. Because when you pay down
American Express, they just add the debt
To the interest. You were stubborn. So they
Kept you right here in New York, the old life.

There I was stuck with maps, spikes to rappel
The bags and the stamps and the sandwiches made
And nothing to do but start on the trail.
I took in the sun as it dazzled and baked me
O my Apollonia! —my desert companion.
I sleep with you now in hot day and cold night
But I cannot kiss you, the desert's so dry.

# Summer Night Poem

Dearly Beloved,
    the air is charcoal
In the summer room. There is molten drama
In the creases of sheets pushed to the edge
Of the bed. I am writing to no one
In the night. The orangutan of dream
Swings through the hooting tulipy treetops
The night is more decent than I am.

The night is more decent than I am
In the way it cares more for me than itself
It wears a neat white shirt and tie
And carries a rolled umbrella should rain
Come pouring into my mouth and drown me
While I am all jungle it is a town
Planned and well kept, gated and shut

Dearly Beloved,
    the gate is charcoal
As if flames had cleansed the wooden lock. One can
Chop off a block and sketch the wanderer
Returning to the gated city again
Under the hooting treetops she enters
The decent house, crawls into creased sheets
And feels rain begin to fall into her mouth

# Winter Night Poem

When life's gruesome and the weather's gruesome
Life's more gruesome. You might mentally review
Your cold weather gear and how much it cost
And with a little quick arithmetic
Convince yourself you actually made money
Buying all that arctic grade outerwear
Because of the many, many times you'll need it.

You might do that. You might take another tack
And dig into your juvenile novel
To reinvent your younger self and it.
Or to reinvent the sad older self
With the experience and consciousness
Gained from the many, many years it has
Taken you to take it out and have a look.

Some just ignore the whole show. They wear six
Layers under their thin spring jackets, wear
Liners under their thin leather gloves, go
Shopping for tropical fruits fearlessly.
They refuse to go under the bed for
The shoebox holding the novel. Whatever.
When the weather is gruesome, life's rough.

Summer Night Poem
Russian Hands


I have no ideas anymore. My hands
Are allayed in gloves or waiting for gloves.
They are stuck, chopped in the hedges.
They are lifting soup to an open mouth.
Grusha! How could you, from any Russian
Novel I have read, peaceably,
Take your hands and rip off both my ears?

I have wandered the tenebrous night streets
Looking for lost hands, my own and others,
And find heaps of them holding each other
Comfortably over the stomach of Time
While the city breathed in and out beneath them.
I—what could I do as not part of
This monster? I was part of something else.

And then there are my own hands, washing some
Dirty part of me and reaching into
My mouth to waggle an old tooth—your tooth,
Grusha! Who from any Russian novel comes
Like a Tolstoy serf with cracked hands
Or Oblomov's hands that didn't do anything
Or Dostoyevsky's hands that barely stayed off his own neck . . . .

# Cuffs

"If I roll these cuffs it makes the uniform
Less uniform." He reformed his pants legs
To make a form that fit the form he was.
A more relaxed and casual man, a man
Who walked where and when he wanted, and a man
Who looked at whom he wanted to look at
With a young man's wanting and not wanting look.

But he was still a man in uniform.
He still took orders, did what he was told.
The crummy blazer gave it all away
He couldn't shrug it off or roll it up
Couldn't leave it hanging on a chair
Or sling it from a casual shoulder. He

Was a man cuffed to job. And sometime
When he is a man standing alone
Holding a baby vomiting all night
There will be no one to give him orders
And he will turn to the mirror and roll
His sleeves up, and there will be freedom in it
And everything else will seem unimportant.

# The Lockjob

Many can sit on a fair sunny day
With lockjob in hand and a great smiling mug
By lockjob I reference wrists bound, mouth gagged
The beautiful normal, the gaudy redress
Of mothers and fathers who mouth us and mold
Us of teachers and trainers who give us tight-
Holding third-wheels and names that mark us as fucked.

I sat by the sailboats with lockjob in hand
Because I'd been literally there, earlier.
Where? In the lockup, the ward, the reward
For feeling quite tragic that Jack had left Jill
And Jill feeling jilted had taken some pills
And Jack called the kind cops to help get her locked
And now all was well as she sat in the lock.

I sat for 12 hours that fine sunny day
With nothing but mom and Jack on my mind
How hijacked I'd been by me mum's gruesome group
Of Motls and Shmuels and Gittels and Leahs,
The dead rising angry and hungry and dead
The dead are so dead oh my darling, so dead
And locked in my heart, oh so locked in my heart.

# Oboe

The moody mythical has been shut down.
Under the oboe player's chipped chewed hands
And from the pale plump opalescent mouth
Fall seven notes into the saltless night
Like seven birds whose wings have been torn off.
In the days of coming reality
Will be people and things real as day.

Meaning, the gloried spoken out will fall
Into a whisper in the mythless night.
Will pour like milk into the waiting ear
Recoiling, though an ear cannot recoil.
Will listen for the sounds beneath the dark
The whole damn orchestra, the galloping thrill
But hear the oboed scale. Those notes will lick

Its underside, poor fleshy thing, poor ear.
The ear is curling in-ness, is a world
That wants the wet surprise of something true.
It sits, a dumpling on each round head's side.
It mourns the end of even oboed notes.
I saw a man with elf ears on the train.
He heard the elf world. I once heard a world.

# The Cure

If kisses were cures and doctors and deans
lived on the fucking paychecks that we do
and dogs loved their leashes and cats their lice
and saints really anybody at all
then we would be living my sweet as one
on an island of savages of love
and we would be savages of love, too.

But kisses are curses and doctors and deans
make money like drug lords and murderers
and dogs chew their legs off and cats their ears
and saints impugn angels with smug small looks
and we are still living apart, as two,
on an island of urban savages
and we are those urban savages, too.

So kiss me now—let's kill them, those horrible shits
who own us and use us like animals.
Like dogs, obedient, like cats, affectionate
they have us both heeling and purring.
Kiss me, and cure me, on our island home
with its buildings and parks and great lit bars
and we'll be those bars, open all night, too.

# Originals

My kimono, which I wore for a beloved
Who does not love me anymore
Is as fresh and beautiful as the night
I hung it covered with a million kisses
On its lining from the neck to the hem.
Each night I kiss one of the kisses
So that I will be loved for a million nights.

When the cyclamen in my garden cycled
Back to their natural notes of iridium, coral
I could hear the nymphs sigh with soft relief
That everything had become normal again.
The beasties with cloven hooves, the hippo
Who tastes like taffy and all the night comets
Sank into sleep in my garden with a sigh.

It's strange but the tiny head of David
Sitting on my desk by a Chinese egg
Has in its neck tendon all of the
Heavy Slavonic homoelectricity
Of the original huge marble thing.
And when I pick it up its tiny lips
Are sealed against kisses, like the real one.

# Summer Night Poem

Now there is no difference between night and day
Night's invaded morning and made great
Encampments all along the city limits
Night's campfires are brighter than the sun
And light afternoons with their afterglow
Even the twilight that slept thigh to thigh
With night is taken captive and laid low

It began, in fact, with the ambush of twilight
Dog soldiers came solemnly over the hours
Silent and grim they relentlessly advanced
Throwing lassoes of darkness around dusk
Muffling soft tinkling laughter over drinks
Silencing last goodbyes, first sweet greetings
And taking them hostage as the sun set

Well, we knew summer's day had had its day
Had pushed its snout too far under night's wing
Had insisted no lights were needed, no
Candles, that kisses were really bright enough
And talk, talking made great day's empire bright
Made day lovely as night whose lingering voice
Now means day never starts, night never ends

# Summer Night Poem

The night the night comes galloping
Awkwardly, it is a handsome giraffe.
Who knows a famous writer we know
Who knows many people we would like to know
He arrives, a visitor we expected
A tall idea loping from the distance
And up the open avenues of late August

It's already August. The botanist
Is already planning future summers
We might have done some things with this summer
Cleaned books, written Shawangunks, dieted like crazy
But instead we did things with this summer
Pretty illicit, almost illegal
We slept in, we puttered around, we swam

We succumbed. We made love to this summer
Held it in our arms through its hundred nights
Smooched it up under its thousand stars
Then closed our eyes, became simpletons of sleep
In our dreams a tower grew like a weed
We climbed it into its thousands of stars
Up, up the giraffe's neck, into the day

# MY HEART
# WAS LIKE A SWORD

# Acknowledgments

## *MY HEART WAS LIKE A SWORD*

"In the Reading Room of the 42nd Street Library," "Semiramis," "Chaucer at Aldgate," "Chaucer at Park House," "Nothing But Margery Kempe," and "King Solomon and Dame Julian in the Nut Garden" appeared in *The Paris Review*.

"My Heart Was Like a Sword" appeared in *Poetry Flash*.

"How Poetry Began" appeared in the online journal, *Switched-on Gutenberg*.

"'Adelaide' at Twilight" appeared in *Blue Unicorn*.

"German Art History, or The Annihilation of *Maria mit Kind*," "Venetian Music," and "God Puts His Hand on Her" appeared in *Dialectical Anthropology: Poetry and Ethics after the Holocaust—a Millennium Memorial*.

# Contents of *My Heart Was Like a Sword*

## *For Me, the World Begins with Doubt*
## *(and Ends with Wonder?)*

# *I Was Also in Arcadia*

# My Heart Was Like a Sword

When I was young my heart was like a sword
that I wore on my sleeve or at my side.
Or, I hid it settled down, slim, thrust in
to the sheath of my body. That red hay
moved when I moved. The bright sword cut both ways.

Certainly I smelled blood; it reached my chin
and spilled out of my mouth and nose and eyes.
People thought I was a killer. They cursed
me, but I was alone with a great thirst
and slayed Spring and the beautiful things first.

Pansies, roses, skin, lips, hips and the sky,
all of it. My heart and the world bled.
Yes, or, I bled on it, quiet thing, blind
metal of my soul. It cut my young brain
into a brilliant bowl where I poured pain

and other things—pleasure for one. Other
things. Just walking around, for instance speared,
suddenly, acute sight, taste; the cool steel
skinned hours, plunged right through their center to steal
words, thoughts, and from the mouths of babes, their meals.

I wore big boots with my sword, a big shout
broke out of me those days. Those days, over
and done. And I don't miss them much although
I hear, dreaming, "Your heart is still a sword."
A gorgeous angel sweetly calls me, "Lord."

# Semiramis

*Lascivis penitus lex est ablata deabus*
When goddesses yield to voluptuousness, law is wholly overcome

from *Semiramis*, an 11th century manuscript found in northern France;
translated by Peter Dronke

In the time it takes for a hummingbird
to scratch his subtle ear, Semiramis
was not "the woman who took Babylon"
but the one who opened her thighs and stretched
for Jove to take his pleasure in the vetch.

See how the god mounts her powerful back
and clasps the warrior thighs in his great loins,
smelling of dung and wild carrots. Rejoice
in the mutual lowing, the mad voice
of interspecies love untethered, moist

flinging off its used shame like a snakeskin
and pressing flesh to flesh—"Who comes back chaste
from the garden, if Jove wills otherwise?"
She shivers. He shudders down. They both breathe,
unoriginal as Adam and Eve.

A woman's honor stained by a bull's loins?
Semiramis laughs from her funeral urn.
But her brother isn't laughing. Her hips
have set tongues against him like cruel whips;
"O sister, bring me your tragic lips!"

he weeps weakly, being a weak, nice boy.
"This is no tragedy," she says, "to love
a god, to be embraced, caressed, inspired
into the urn. Catch on now, or never . . .
the dead are not granted speech forever."

# How Poetry Began

*vidi ipsum materno sanguine nasci*
I saw him born from his mother's blood

Ovid, *Metamorphoses*, Book V

"I saw the horse born from his mother's blood,"
Minerva mentions to Urania,
laying her helmet on Mt. Helicon's
grass, spangled with flowers. She refuses
a cold drink from one of the Muses

passing her muscled forearm through the spring
struck open by Pegasus' sharp front hoof.
She drips its water on her sunburnt neck.
She feels in her goddess thighs the long trek
and remembers, unwillingly, that wreck.

That upright torso. And there was the head
hissing and spitting from a distance. Snakes
writhed around two bright shocked eyes. A red mouth
like a rosebud wailed against ancient teeth
uttering nonsense; she saw how beneath

the hero hand, it hung like a sausage.
It kept calling for its lost body, blood
leaped up from it, fell into the lagoon—
smoky, sulphurous—something winged soon
writhed out of all the gore and rank ruin

of the Gorgon—a great winged, white horse came
sauntering here . . . Pallas opens her eyes.
"I cannot bear," she says, "to miss a song
from dear Calliope. Let's not wait.
The art's already begun; she is late."

## In the Reading Room
## of the 42nd Street Library

These good New Yorkers bent low over books
deserve a Paradise of softer chairs
and sleep, their heads against that fringed and white
length of swan neck, spotless, damp, sleek, warm
to recover on, after a god's form

has entered and taken them willingly
thoroughly, and with great, big, tender sighs.
They deserve that mythic neck, a Christian
heaven, the upliftings of good fiction,
cushioned seats, and sweet poetic dictions.

But softly one hears, from almost still lips:
"They no longer pasture on new meadows."
Then, "Poets sound like salesmen, talk show hosts . . ."
"Who's *'molle atque facetum'*? Speak!—
wonderful human—from the mountain peak . . ."

They mumble this from their vast, troubled ooze
of dream, as the dusty light filters in.
Only in their fragile sleep a singer
reappears, the notes begin to linger
and sound, only here time's scraping finger

begins to carve some worthwhile heap of words
to scatter widely for a swan's return
to paint the visionary dreariness
to light the dawn coming up like thunder
that breaks like ice down the face of wonder.

# This Little Father of Winter

This little red-cloaked father of winter
who comes ministerially in his plumes
has a dark eye. He looks with his dark eye.
He ignores a soft, various sunbeam
and eats his food emitting thin, hot steam

from his beak. It is hard even to think
that Romance pours from such a sullen lip
or that his heart, dense as a white pebble,
is the source and the spring of a treble
so high-pitched, so piercing sweet it levels

mere novelty. But he's an old, old act.
Out of the winter, out of the lamby
language of winter all bleat and scared whine
come the little births of sharp and good things
that are useful and bright, like knives and rings

and they have this red mister as father.
For their mother, the wind's practicing hand.
So then, what will be the children of light?
Who will launch them out of approaching night
into all their days of warmth and delight?

You Tityrus? You who kept all your lands
while ours were burnt down by the gods, and men?
You old shepherd? Or some new big-mouthed boys?
Or will it be a bird out of season
who opens their hearts to love and reason?

# The Owls at Number Nineteen

This is a night poem, a poem of the night
written at midnight in the countryside
out of darkness, that is, the loneliness
of riding at night on a bus through strange
landscapes which in the dark are out of range

of sensual eye scanning the windows
for landmarks, or for anything at all
since leaving the last lighted city street
with its mobile, warm gaiety, its neat
windows there like loving, lived-in eyes, seats

of London's soul, great eyeballs in gauzy
silks or damask and lamplit, bloodshot, soft.
It's a poem about the last lit site:
It was an entrance to a sort of park
or large house, quiet, without a dog's bark

or mewling peacock to guard it (city
houses don't have dogs that bark, in London,
or peacocks, that's for the country) but two
tall tapering columns almost imbued
with white, more than painted white, not a true

white but shadowed with dull blue like veinblood
running under skin, and in the same milk-
blue color two owls, cloaked in dark leaves,
shiny, like gardenia's leaves, glowed and preened
above the quickly daubed address, Nineteen.

## "Adelaide" at Twilight

Out of a radio's bewildered throat,
out of the falling dark and through bare trees
tumbles the sweetest tune, to me, to me
sitting down as though a hand put me there
to wait for Adelaide to appear

again, as she once appeared before, high
on a hill with tears glittering, spilling,
and breath caught, and a shawl wrapped around her
and the earth caught in wonder surrounds her
and creation, all tenderness, bounds her

with blue sky, cobalt, finally red sky
flames up like her lover's hope up the hill
as he runs to clasp her and embrace her
but nowhere, nowhere can he find his love
in the twilight. Look, the murmuring dove

finds her home, but nowhere are the lovers
home, always parted by the centuries
and me from them, and from young Beethoven
all soul and longing and in love with them,
and the love of the singer, young Bjoerling.

All of them young but oldness beginning,
and deafness, and death, and Adelaide
lost in the tender notes covering me
like a cloak in the twilight, in the night—
and I hear her come to come, come to me . . .

# *Mythical and Historical People I've Known*

# Chaucer at Aldgate

Late in the century, Chaucer stretches
having just finished with his reckonings
in wool, checking them all against the chits
of rich and cunning men like Philipot
and Bembre (seeing what passes, and not)

before blotting down the columns of ink—
he closes the book with a pursed lip
and glances from the custom house window
he gets up, saunters outside (an elbow
of velvet freshening the stones, set low)

finally he makes his way to Aldgate,
and finally sits at *another book.*
It is his book, and each book is a house,
each made within the gated city wall
which houses, too, the poet's musing hall

long and luxurious and always filled
with lover's doubts, a fallen maiden's tears
Latin consolations, what bright birds said
squawking over love, the echoing tread
of famous heroes rising from the dead.

The customhouse is a small, simple spot
for all of its dumbshow of knowingness
men trade, men cheat, men hoard for King and self—
but worlds are coming, raucous and devout
as Chaucer, pale at Aldgate, writes them out.

# Chaucer Leaving Aldgate

Why pale? I already hear the complaints—
this poet isn't dreamy and white-skinned,
isn't torn with self-consciousness or doubt,
isn't pale—isn't begging for a prize,
passing quite easily before men's eyes.

But have *you not seen sometimes a pale face,*
having hidden thoughts in a winter wood
only to look up at a sudden sun
and find below, everywhere, at a run,
hate: the Rising of 1381?

The poet looks down, sees a flood of men
pulsing beneath him like a tide of blood
and blood they are, and England's blood at that.
And looking down, he sees with no surprise
those looking up are looking with men's eyes.

Soon everyone is feeling Saturn's hand,
bishop, Fleming, all sorry islanders.
This smiling is the father of pestilence,
this ruining he does with diligence,
this thought is the emptying of all sense

from the universe. Soon Chaucer will leave,
as sanguine, seasoned men will make their way
right to the noose, and the undoing of kings.
Nicolas Bembre, collector, will die
his soft boots glittering in a bleared eye.

# Chaucer at Park House

And here we are at last in the forest,
green, a depth of green seen from a saddle,
the horse under it steaming, stops. Closed nose,
a trumpet opens. His foamed mouth, a sack,
sucks up green water out of the brown muck.

The poet sits quietly looking around.
Then galloping, galloping, galloping
out of his old age, into the sweet reply
everywhere darting like a dragonfly,
(wings scratching against an astonished sky)

something starts up, hovering in the air—
so Chaucer lightly holds his pen aloft—
scratches his head, unbottles both his ears—
and hears something near getting very loud,
very ardent, caressing—a great crowd

spills into the meadow. They sit around
the poet's feet and around his two arms,
eyes, head, heart. Chaucer reaches to a leaf.
How smooth it is, and what a relief
the horse has in making a meal so sweet.

The horse munches, casting a slow horse eye
on the pilgrims arriving now and then
and settling in under the great trees.
Here, deep in the enigmatic forest,
Chaucer welcomes himself as the last guest.

# Nothing But Margery Kempe

*"Alas that ever did I sin! It is full merry in Heaven!"*
*The Book of Margery Kempe*

Think of Margery Kempe, who laughed and cried
while worshipping along the grassy walks,
who sought salvation with an open heart
and nothing but her mouth turned up or down
to prove her faith to a bishop or crown.

Did she carry a staff? Wear otter shoes?
And a hat of brick filled with tousled sweat?
Did she carry a purse with a barb or pearl?
One might guess that the agony that swirled
in the midst of her mirth was her bond with the world.

Consider Margery comic, also
consider her as she loved her husband—
desperately, with physical passion
so that nothing but her legal desire
threatened to put her into the fire.

She feared hell, loved heaven, and the angel's tooth
that gnaws away the flesh with temperance—
think of this woman, who was half a saint,
that the yearning for God could make her faint
in the midst of laughing off life's gross taint.

It's enough to make others laugh and cry
when someone is doing it all the time—
who has a husband so in love that he
doesn't seem to mind. One could laugh, and cry—
until in the natural way, one died.

# In the Woods with Richard Rolle

Let's watch the future mystic reach into
his father's things left drying in the hall.
He fingers the authoritative gear
and alarmed by faith, shoves it down his cape
and makes his irrevocable escape

into the woods. He sits on a damp rock.
His sister comes down the leafy path
carrying two dresses, one white, one grey
as agreed upon the previous day
humming softly. She turns away

for a minute. She turns back and stops short.
He has torn one sleeve from her fine grey dress
and is at work on the other. He rips
the buttons off the white. He looks up, beams.
She gasps. "My brother has gone mad!" she screams.

"But no," says Richard putting on the hood
that was his father's rainhat, as a cowl.
He stands before her dressed in her own forms
which with rough hands he has wholly reformed
remade himself, or God remade, transformed

into a future hermit, now a boy
down from Oxford for the long vacation
forced to surrender temporarily
his will, incendiary love, the dresses
his future greatness, his future messes.

# Julian's Toilette

"And all will be well, and all will be well. . ."
*Revelations of Divine Love,* Dame Julian of Norwich, 1373

"All manner of things shall be well. . ."
*Little Gidding,* T.S. Eliot, 1943

This is the day, so freshly born again
with robins singing heavily. And moles
burrowing the ends of the lettuce crop.
Through a Cross in the screen the sunlight flares
on Julian, anchoress, at prayers.

Though even before, when the moon's crescent
tongued light over fallow Christian fields
there was the weeping of brooms over stone,
the wrenching agony of water's groan
in the bucket, and wailing human bone

sunk under the white flesh of good women.
Julian's two, grim, plain-faced maiden dames
were rinsing off their necks, underarms, toes
before bringing more water and a cloth
to Julian, white as a cabbage moth

and waiting patiently, palms on her knees . . .
Although this was the earliest hour
for tending to the rising body's needs
and clothing its appalling frailties
flesh was not only grossness, rank disease

to Julian. One time, at four a.m.,
she saw the Lord Christ, bleeding on the Cross
and found her calling. She became a voice.
A thing apart. Our Great High-Modern bard
stopped late, to watch the chickens in the yard.

## King Solomon and Dame Julian
## in the Nut Garden

Through the veiled hush of the nut garden, God
was walking in the cool of the day; He
felt like talking again to a mortal
being, someone bright, maybe a king, who
might listen for once, but that would be too

wonderful, really, by a long shot, yet
he sought one of them out, Solomon, who
was wise and kind and a very fair man.
Later Solomon would say he began
"descending" in order to understand—

going down, "penetrating" the garden.
Impatiently peeling the layered shells
of the nuts, he would claim to know new things
about the cosmos, how the soul of light
lay deep at the core of the mystic night.

Then, much later, an eyeblink later, God
wanted to speak again with a mortal
being, someone bright, maybe a woman
off on the side somewhere who'd understand
the nuts in the garden, how it began

with a nut and ended up as a
Universe, although nothing had changed much
except size. And He handed Julian
the nut. She said, "It is all that is made.
Love keeps it safe." And God paused as she prayed.

# *Signs from God and Nature*

# God Puts His Hand on Her

The hand of God is on her and she shakes,
just like Abraham. He sits on a hill,
and looks down on the milky wilderness,
and shakes. He cries out to his little son,
"You are the sacrifice, unlucky one."

Easier to be Moses on the bank,
left behind while his tribe goes to safety.
A flushed Joshua calls, "Everyone crosses!"
But he can't. He lifts his hand and tosses
voluntary farewells to future losses.

Better to be Judith with a bright sword
hung over the enemy. Better—best.
She stands there, great, in rigid arabesque.
She swaddles her lover in a hot shroud.
She leaves his bloody head for a shocked crowd.

More like Abraham, more like poor Hagar
who drags her bastard child through the desert,
sneering, "Thou art Ishmael, let no man
do anything but strike you with his hand
or heel—and God hates you like the sand

which is too numerous to count or love."
Oh little suffering dove, child, flower
released into the classroom of her thoughts,
you rise like Nature's hottest, vengeful breath,
spit out of that One's cold magnificence.

# O, Invisible Birds

O, invisible birds who sing for spring
who sing much louder than the mouths of men
who sing much higher, sweeter than the one
who sits stopped-throated, gong-songed near the tree
finding no way into the melody.

O, invisible birds who sing for spring
who sing continuously, without end
who sing riotously, ringing out song
banishing nothingness, time that feels long
and that little murmurer, bitter, wrong.

Their songs are bright, like the world without stop,
like the world that spins through both time and dark
bright—as if the sun broke off and got stuck
within the narrow gullets of the birds
who burst their hearts to utter without words.

They sing against that singer who has stopped,
that sad myself. Some optimist says, wait.
The birds are busy, listen and you'll hear
rustlings, movements, plans muttered in an ear
sculpted out of greenness, tier after tier.

Then, rising like the hope that we all find work
as easily as birds do, a large black crow
lifts a heavy branch in her cold black beak.
She goes to build a nest of some great size
far off, high up, and hidden in the skies.

# Nest

In the evening a robin builds a nest.
There is nothing sentimental in this
description, statement of fact, introduction
to a description of activity
or, actually, in the activity.

In fact, there is a flat banality
to the words and lack of images—no:
"*a bird ascends.*" Actually it did
like a living cross, flew up in a bid
for romantic Immortality. Hid

and dropped a piece of extra straw, a stick . . .
Plenitude falling down from an extra
fine and azure field, a bright swollen Breast
spilling all its extraness on the ground
in a pantomime of phantom limb—sound

only a rustle, a squeak, then a slap,
a battering at my head swinging back, up
and again, again, cracked by the unseen
Hand, whipped harshly by the powerful, lean
arm of the Driver of Souls—poor, small, mean

me in the midst of the chaos of Goodness . . .
or was I? Wasn't I just sitting there
 in the slum of summer evening, drinking,
and a bird was doing something equal
to prayer and also with a sequel?

# I Held the Key

I held the key to all things in my hand
or at least, in my head, and kept it there
for a while not worrying about time
or forgetfulness; and then I forgot.
It was all lost in a minute, a slot

in time had opened and my penny fell
down into the deep and then disappeared.
Although I once tried looking for its shine
up from below, its sparkle in the brine,
I drew the darkness over it, a sign

that I'd known nothing very important
if it could slip from me in a minute
and sit there on the bottom of the earth,
sidling up to fishes, up to snakes, shells,
coral, and lay itself in sand, a cell

of something, a particle of reason
sunk to nothing, out of sight, out of mind
and certainly, finally, utterly
gone. Well, I'd lost it. And quite carelessly.
I felt pretty bad, in fact an old tree

couldn't have felt more rooted in its spot—
and not an upright tree, one turned over
and growing with its stormy roots stuck in,
eternally decaying in some park
where drunks curl up, contented, in the dark.

# German Art History,
## or The Annihilation of *Maria mit Kind*
(1476-1486)

*The low relief shows a girlish figure*
*standing next to the profiled architec-*
*tonic framing, holding a little child*
*at present, almost entirely missing. . .*
This much we know from the current listing.

Also, that although the child is gone
it was clearly meant to show the sweet pair
near a crashing Idol. But we arrive
too late to see the Infant, burned alive
in the bombings of nineteen forty-five.
.  .  .  .
Then there is Die Synagogue of Beckman
where one can yet view the *trumpet-blowing*
*Ugi Battenberg, his wife Fridel, Max. . .*
*all merry-making at the hour of prayer*
*while an elder warns, hand raised in the air.*

Perhaps that the National Socialists
will burn down the temple in '38?
as the Allies will bomb in '44?:
Here was an angel; yet there was the door;
there were the pellets that hissed to the floor.
.  .  .  .
As the Idol remakes its abject form
and rises on limbs that rattle and creak,
the raised hand is again consumed by fire.
Ah marvelous lost world! Never remade,
annihilated like the simple shade.

(Quotations are from a sample art history entry,
handed out in a German Level I class)

# O *Nehushtan!* in My Patch

O *Nehushtan!* in my garden patch
doth smilingly adore the day's first heat—
remember that in Hezekiah's reign
he broke the brazen serpent Moses made
because it pleased the Lord to whom he prayed!

In that first garden, *nachash*—tempting Eve
to tempt her husband with a piece of fruit,
even their children's children are reviled—
and there in that first garden patch you smiled,
our mother whispering, "Lord, I was beguiled."

As *saraph* you were sent to sting the mob
who crossed with Moses towards the Red Sea.
Setting out from Mount Hor, they found just sand
and little else. They cursed aloud and cried.
Then God sent you. Lo, many of them died.

And read in Matthew; there's the constant wail,
"You brood of vipers!" as if every saint
used your foul name from Rome to Galilee
"Brood of vipers!" (John to the Sadducees).
"You vipers!" (Jesus to the Pharisees).
    (see more in Matthew 3, 12, 23)

But from the shipwreck you once salvaged Paul
by posing as a bracelet on his wrist
so that the men of Malta stood aghast
and thought he was a god, and heaven sent
and lifted him with incense to their tents.

# Begun at Woodlawn Cemetery

Here's a dogwood, there's a huge chestnut tree
spiraling up its pearly, moody woodnotes.
Here ivy embraces the breathless breast
and the walls of houses are thick and strong.
Why, since man's poor meat blackens and then rots
do the dead deserve such very nice spots?

Does every open field cry "O, return!"
(Return, return; and take up residence.)
Its expanse an invitation: plant feet
either live ones, Gucci-booted and neat
or splay-toed corpses, prodigal and deep.

A wild field is a good thing for the eye:
finds itself traveling down and rolling up—
carries the hard mind to some softer zone
the hard heart from its center, sets it free
for a swim into general memory.

A pheasant needs an entire field to mate—
he or she is satisfied to share space
with deer, a herd of turkeys—but its kind
must pick another field—they cannot mind—
that is the pheasant way and comes to bind

all pheasants yea even unto the tenth
generation. Look, I can remember
a ravishing field, near the house. With all
its wings, beaks, hooves, still, like a dreaming sea
it tossed its young head, both full and empty.

# *People I've Met*

# Three Beggars

The streets are full of men who beg for things,
money, or cigarettes, or things to eat.
They're new, a quiet sedentary group
who lift their faces from the centuries
of kindness for those beaten to their knees.

They sit so sadly in the afternoon,
they move you. Although some gave more to a
large broad, mythic Nemesis who struck
his stick down subway cars demanding luck
and whom they watched before the doors unstuck:

a modern, unrepentant public self
he took it as his job to strike the floor,
remind the earth, and all earth's audience
that need could walk upright, become a man,
and be crowned king of tentless caravans.

And then there's still the lecher with his cup
who sits outside the Presbyterian church.
He looks up skirts, he wheedles for his share,
his face is tan, his body shows the care
he spends on his own fairest of the fair.

But Herbert, with his pale and dreadful arm,
belongs to that new army of the whipped
who have been hit and stitched and sent back out
to raise his youthful eyes to a sublime
that has, like hunger, endless space and time.

# The Fish Who Smokes

*El pez que fuma* is the fish who smokes
a long and fragrant pipe to advertise
a restaurant. He assumes three postures:
reclining on a beach, then quite upright,
then swimming in a blue and tropic light.

To see this fish is to be brought at once
into island dreams of rice and red beans
and conversations that go all night long
over cigarettes as an island song
comes wafting under the tumbling dawn.

Tumbling down Park Avenue—the clouds
grey and naked as they start to splash about
an undogmatic trail of shining drops
sprinkle the boulevard and the dark
along 125th and Park.

As the sleepless hitch up their trouser pants
or open a button at an old neck's
soft and buttery skin, one hears them say,
"Behold la noche sliding into day"
as the El train begins to make its way

leaving the arc of the thoroughfare
inscribed by the people now gathering
at corners to cross and recross and then pause
thinking of breakfast and the tireless folk
who simmer the dawn at The Fish Who Smokes.

# Summer

It was the end of June. The great puffed heads
of salsify stood sentinel to our
orb whose urban twin was peeking into
Manhattan's chasms, peering down along
uniform boulevards of Sturm und Drang

while we were in the country enjoying
the mild eye of Phoebus scanning our cheeks
and Zephyr ladling ruffs of kisses—
watery—over mister and missus
of burp cavorting low over fishes

only to be swallowed whole, still kicking,
by the green-backed heron in his splendor . . .
and we were all being eaten alive,
by late May flies and hot young mosquitoes
lusting for the dumb, ingenuous nose

of a newcomer—and we were planning
what to eat next and what to have to drink
and letting our hands drift along the grass
rippling in the wind-wake's rough aftermath
as our heads spun in and out of the past

reviewing where we'd left our shoes, the word
we'd spoken that set off such a rupture
suddenly, everything smashed and gone wrong.
And as suddenly forgotten, over,
the dogs affably asleep in clover.

# Venetian Music

O place of palaces and Veronese!
Venice in her backwash of foetid waves
has bred a music made of ends and means.
Out of her tides, out of her reeking spill
up music splashed like Venus, loved and willed.

My poor rabbi. He stands alone, talking.
What does he have to put on the table?
What can he use to bargain for our ears?
Gabrielli Giovanni gave us fear,
sweetness, a Virgin birth. What we have here

on the other hand is a bearded man
in a dark suit, tie not unstained, having
rushed out from a quick meal in a kosher
pizza parlor, where he's met a lost soul
lost, lulled, lullabyed and cajoled

by Venetian music into sighing
for a Savior of mild, beautiful limbs
for whom she'll be a butterfly of song
gathered up in His arms and brought along
up high, high into the elegant, long

Italian sunset of blues and soft golds . . .
O that her ear could but hear! The rabbi
alone, standing, talking, savoring how hard
Rabbi Akiba worked to make the deal
for a glimpse of the throne, the heat of the wheel.

# Proust and Ritual Slaughter

"Consider the one circumstance that no Jewish mother ever killed a chicken with her own hand, and you will understand why homicide is rarer among Jews."
A. Lerory Beaulieu, *Soncino Chumash* commentary, p. 487

I saw Kristeva speak in London once
on Proust, after lunch at the Oriel
and a drink with a wealthy Englishman
who had written something. Would write some more.
Had searched the East for some god to adore.

Verily, a pilgrim heart in pinstripes.
Had an income from investments and owned
a house in Knightsbridge, one in Surrey, too.
Invitations predictably ensued
extended, for form, to a New York Jew.

Then he asked, if the Messiah appeared
wouldn't one make a mad dash for the door?
Perhaps, I demurred. But perhaps the light
flooding from those deep and hungering eyes
would make us tyros leap, to be God's spies.

Perhaps. He sighed a little at his wine.
Had once, in fact, given orders a go.
C of E had proved a bit of a washout—
not much to hang onto in the fleshpots
so to speak. And he waved, smiling me out

the door and into the curious crowd.
Later, a small Moroccan Jew explained
as we took the Tube: Proust's mere Jewishness
was provocation, like one's being queer,
for wonder, the chambers, the well-bred sneer.

# Lines for Geri

(about last things, drinking, and gardening,
ending on a note of whimsy)

I thought of you when I saw the sunset
and how one day we'll both be taken up
into the soft bosom of the clouds, wrapped
in a scarf of eternity and blue
unbound, unbound at last! and me from you . . .

That day of splendor will be saddest
of all, even if we slip between shades
of unremitting orange, of slate grey
and hear the adorable angels play—
if it means that all the things that we say

are last things. Then it's not really worth it.
Because there is always much more to say
exiting to the drama of the streets
after a drink, and the words languishing
still, on the corners of stone, brandishing

a sword of meaning against formlessness,
and the cool flesh of twilight . . . And still more
to salute with the next raised drink or spade
anticipating, in the dappled shade,
the glorious future of that green glade

that looks like an ordinary garden
but is a little wonder to us both—
here's a toast to the finch, as darkness comes
to the sparrows, the jays, with whom arrive
chariots of elves, and the leprechaun's bride . . .

# An Old Woman

I met an old woman who was a poem
over-rouged, garrulous and insulting
something Restoration and overdone,
self-consciously old, quite grotesque, bereft—
something read, memorized, performed and left.

I met an old woman who was a poem
as they are, touched by Immortality
and the sweetness of our own faded days
and the longings of our wandering ways
through the lens of time, the romantic haze.

I met an old woman who was a poem
sitting on a bench near the library
in the cold, with a bag of bread, rye bread
because she likes rye bread, the Jewish rye.
She liked eating it in the park nearby.

I met an old woman who was a poem
shuddering, escaped from her hotel lift
where ale-dry she'd tucked up her sad curled hair
in her hat, and prayed that from anywhere help
would come in a form noble and fair.

I met an old woman who was a poem
because she had lived the large, other life
which is the dreaming life made palpable.
First out on the ice on her skates in her youth
and then later with pigeons, gin, and vermouth.

# *For Me,*
# *the World Begins with Doubt*
# *(and Ends with Wonder?)*

# Half Moon Street

I was coming up Half Moon Street and I
wasn't half surprised to be less than half
pleased with the heat; here it was, God, London
and eleven at night, and still the tune
was New York. Of course there was a half-moon

up Hays Mews as I wandered looking for
Lalani's, the late-night deli I knew
there—I ran on, the hum of the plane still
lilting in my veins, spotting down the hill
the little shop opening like a rill

sparkling with Perrier and Evian
and all things wet and wonderful—I bought
three bottles. In front of the restaurant
called Zen Center one bottle fell out, hit
the pavement and spun around spurting spit

and hissing. Then I stopped and I wondered
will it explode? Will the hot English night
be shattered as the smiling neat doorman
of Zen Center, hearing the roar and grand
sputter of it comes lunging, all form and

concern? And will he get hurt, or even
a passerby, a child, a dog, or cat?
Because that's the way my mind works, how it
conjures up genies of remorse and pain
out of a June night in a London lane.

## Wendover Court

One is leaving London, one is going
to the Hall with its garden, and children
laughing from swings tied to venerable oaks.
They are laughing and showing great white teeth
as are rare in High or on the heath.

Then on the M4 it suddenly looms
up, an icon in the dieselish air—
Wendover Court! Like a lozenge of gold
at the bus window. Do the very old
peer from the curtains? Of the slick, the bold?

Will this evocative building get smashed
when the highway is widened? And with it,
ghosts of the 30s from when it was built
and the 50s whose sad spirits attend
Vera Lynn as once more their way they wend?

Yes, it's finished. The geezers, touts, and cons
give over to the weary vacationers
reporting to spires dreaming aloft.
O Oxford! Your students, rosy and soft,
are backdrops for tourists, tired, with coughs.

One stops at the Covered Market before
heading out to the Hall. One's head full of
colts and cows and sweet summer strawberries.
Suddenly, the rich stinking smell of blood:
cut meat, like Wendover Court, out of love.

# On Viewing the Keats
# Bicentenary Exhibit
# at the Grolier Club

(November, 1995)

We should all have seen this small exhibit
when we were 25, even younger—
those of us with sad and beautiful eyes
and tremulous lips could have paused and then
regretfully retired to break our pens.

Once around the room would have been enough.
We'd have been pretty glad to just get out,
having read how at Leigh Hunt's a review
plunged poor, tattered Keats into such a stew
he burst a blood vessel. Could have been you

or me—has been—heart attacks and cancer
lay us just as low as TB did Keats.
He died in a sweat coughing up his blood.
"I do not think my health will improve
much while I am separated from you,"

he wrote to Fanny, who didn't write back,
having chosen a healthier and wealthier
guy. No worse than Shelley who saw the waste
but mentioned Keats' "wretched and narrow taste"
in a note to Byron that reeks of caste.

"I wish I was either in your arms full
of faith or that a thunderbolt would strike
me. God help you." Keats, in his last despair.
Young poets with even a little scope
can render the meaning, "Abandon hope."

# The Senator of Sleep

Tonight my mind's a senator of sleep
unrecognized, just, pale, dignified, dumb.
It lives inside a nation of alerts
lawless, loud, violent, toothed, torn, aroused;
who shout it down, laughing in its own house.

It's invited these visitors to see
its grief. It has displayed itself, has spread
its arms to a hostile bunch of young punks
and makes a row of military bunks
spruce and clean, for them to lie on, get drunk

and yell, "Great white shining wonder of night,
what good is all your reflexiveness now?"
And my mind, it gets up on its hind legs
and pounds its paw for silence, and gets none.
But—that's not true. Let's just leave it alone

or see it for what it is—it doesn't
salute like a general, or stand up,
a legislator in the unruled flesh;
it's knit with all of me—it makes my mesh
and is me and makes me and begs me: "Bless

me, bless me lest I crush us on a whim."
It's a battlefield where everyone's lost.
And, like some dragon's teeth sown in a dream,
the soldiers rise again on the wide field
to be hacked apart from the next yield.

# As a Woodchuck

When I come back, when my gay molecules
have finished cavorting through the starry
spheres, though the spheres still tinkle with their notes...
maybe, when the sun slants down October
I'll pop up in the grass, give a sober

look at the hill, the field, the country road
and feel a furry new existence start
in my mammal heart, in my rodent brain,
knowing zed of longing or future pain,
lost in the pleasure of the late sun's train

of glory spreading over the meadows
and I might snortle in small Queen Anne's Lace
mingled with chicory, vetch and pinecones . . .
acorns bouncing off the great Shawangunk rise . . .
then, with a sort of wild, marmot surmise

my mouth might fall on flowers and other
edible frills of the earth . . . sweet grasses
and sudden mushrooms . . . ah, so much to chew
and such short days as Fall scatters its clues
about the earth ending, about the dew

freezing on the rose . . . woodchucks descending
into a profound, malodorous sleep . . .
How I will leap out in March with a cry!
How Spring will butter me with kisses!
How I will find it utterly delicious!

# The End of the Day

On a bright day, from under the black boughs,
a golden distance glitters from the hills.
There is a gold horse, a gold goat, a lamb
all shining, off in the distance, each one
shimmering in the rays of a spent sun.

And you could go up and touch each gold head
to receive a look both soft and refined.
Sweetness would come from the depths of six eyes,
as well as the dog's, whose sole enterprise
is to run and lick the gold undersides.

A peaceful kingdom lies there on the hill.
In the yard off to the side of the house
two men are wrestling, off at some distance.
They're tawny gold. They're equal in height,
as well as look and dress; they face to fight.

In the fragrant shade under the black boughs,
each grasps the other's neck, assumes a stance,
and then they move heavily in one way—
And then they move heavily, and they sway—
and they shift and shift, wearing grass to clay

until one topples the other to the ground
and he gets up, and they begin again.
You almost feel the warmth off their bodies
in the night air; the night's lingering smile
widens, breathing mortality a while.

# Lullabye

Everything slows at the end of the day
even the winding internal reflux
slows and subsides, and the blood quiets, too.
Even the eye gets tired and closes,
even the ardent young heart reposes.

Nothing stops, it just changes its temper
and loses some heat in the depths of the dark.
The uniform sky lies wide, like the sea,
and Blueblack unfurls both wind and lee,
a flag of the fallen, those who agree

that heads are meant to fling back with a sigh
and hands to lie open with palms outspread
and chins to tilt to the curving pillow
and knees to rest lightly on the cover
the sleeper released from any other.

Then hand over hand, up the rope of heaven
or foot by foot down the ladder of salt,
the sleeper begins. The wandering blood,
salty as seaweed and slow as the mud,
goes tumbling onward like Noah's flood.

And reasoning closes its stubborn flower,
and wants and desires relax their folds,
as everything slows at the end of the day.
A dreamer might wake in star-blazed brine,
untied from the push and the pull of time.

# On the Forms in this Collection

William Blake famously wrote, "I must create a system or be enslaved by another man's." For me this applies to style and form. Style is an elusive matter, but form is a basic element of poetry. We experience it in oral and written work, ancient and contemporary. Yet though we are often taught sonnets and sestinas in school as set and fixed forms, we know they aren't. Poetry resists imposition. Form has to operate as a gift. It was during one of my innumerable viewings of *Saturday Night Fever* that I noticed John Travolta and his friends walked in iambs in the opening frames, in counterpoint to the disco dactyls and ornate trochees of the Bee Gees. These rhythms and vocalizations come out of our hands and mouths because they are in our bodies; they are in our bodies because we learn a mother tongue.

A major influence on the forms in this collection arose from my immersion in medieval literature. Returning to New York City, I decided that in order to avoid forever the ebullient soul-eating commercialism of my natal city, I'd get a PhD and live in a tower. My initial attempt at creating a form out of this material resulted in the poems collected here as *My Heart Was Like A Sword*, poems from the late eighties and nineties which sometimes take as subjects medieval writers: Julian of Norwich, Margery Kempe, Richard Rolle, Chaucer. Each poem has five stanzas of five lines, with alternating stanzas closing with couplets and triadic rhymes. Each verse is decasyllabic, sometimes scanning into metric feet.

There is number theory behind these choices. For the medieval mind, numbers were not only used to count, but were themselves principles. The number one is not truly a number; it is monadic unity, or God. Therefore two, which in the natural world is the generative pair, is for the Christian mind a falling away from perfection into mutability, the created and fallen world. Certainly hovering just beneath this cardinal understanding lies the shadow of the juicy boy-girl pairing—a tension exploited by Chaucer in *Parliament of Birds* in every plot twist and poetic structure. However, the fall from unity is still the foremost meaning of two—a fall restored by the first "real" hence "male" number: three.

Three is a world-building number because in geometry it constructs the first plane (two points give you a line—three make a triangle which can be further manipulated to render a three-dimensional space). And together threes and twos make five, which in medieval thought elicits Christ's five wounds, the Virgin's five joys, the five human senses. Those who have read *Gawain and the Green Knight* will remember that his shield displays the never-ending five-pointed pentangle, which for all its unifying powers cannot protect him from being caught out in his human imperfections.

My next form was simpler and built on a number not only endowed with mystical meaning but also firmly embedded in the natural world: seven. This number is more closely in touch with Jewish text and tradition. Generally the poems in *Speak in the Dark* have three stanzas of non-rhyming decasyllables of seven lines each. Seven has a spectacular genealogy as the unit of Biblical creation as well as the weekly life-experience of each person trotting blithely under a morphing moon. Each day and night are a discrete enactment of the full yearly turn, but I will leave it to the reader to find her and his own macro and micro readings of the poems' many days and nights, of nature created and creating, and the ongoing annihilations and regenerations of love and war. It might be helpful to know that my mother survived the European war as a Belgian "in hiding," while my father, her liberator, was a fourth-grade drop-out, salesman, and self-taught neo-expressionist from Brooklyn. When I was four or five, my mother and I watched the early news. Suddenly there was footage of the liberation of the camps. The images of the prisoners passed though her mercury into my formlessness. Therefore I am not only a joyful Gemini post-war baby, but a tomb for all the Leahs and Menchels who populate these poems. Everything is a mouth within one asking for language. I want to give them strong syllables. Forms provide all of us, like the little bee in Wordsworth's sonnet "Nuns Fret Not," a bell in which to furiously buzz.

Cynthia Kraman
October 2008
Charles Street, NYC

About the Poet
# Cynthia Kraman

Cynthia Kraman (a.k.a. Cynthia Genser . . . Cynthia Kraman Gen-
ser . . . Chinas Comidas) is the author of three volumes of poetry. Her
first book, *Taking on the Local Color*, was the Wesleyan New Poets Se-
ries selection for 1976. She developed an early version of spoken arts
in Seattle, and published *Club 82* with Workingman's Press in 1979.
At that time she also started a band with Rich Riggins called Chinas
Comidas, whose retrospective CD has received enthusiastic reviews.
While traveling between New York and the West Coast, a collection of
non-syntactic poems and a sonnet series was brought together by e.g.
booksellers & publishers as *The Mexican Murals* in 1986. Her work has
been widely published in literary journals including *The Paris Review,
The Southern Review, How/ever,* and *Open City,* and in anthologies in-
cluding the ground-breaking *Ordinary Women* (1974), *New York: Po-
ems* (Avon 1980), and *Bowery Women: Poems* (Bowery Books 2006).
   She is still fond of her youthful entry for *Contemporary Authors*
where she noted that she was "trying to be a writer a woman a hu-
man being at a time when those are all considered criminal activi-
ties." Cynthia Kraman holds a doctorate in medieval literature from
University of London, Queen Mary. She lives in New York City.

Printed in the United States
215003BV00001B/8/P

9 780980 050882